First World War
and Army of Occupation
War Diary
France, Belgium and Germany

25 DIVISION
74 Infantry Brigade
Alexandra, Princess of Wales's Own (Yorkshire Regiment)
9th Battalion
1 September 1918 - 28 February 1919

WO95/2247/2

The Naval & Military Press Ltd
www.nmarchive.com
Published in association with The National Archives

Published by

The Naval & Military Press Ltd

Unit 10 Ridgewood Industrial Park,

Uckfield, East Sussex,

TN22 5QE England

Tel: +44 (0) 1825 749494

www.naval-military-press.com

www.nmarchive.com

This diary has been reprinted in facsimile from the original. Any imperfections are inevitably reproduced and the quality may fall short of modern type and cartographic standards.

© **Crown Copyright**
Images reproduced by permission of The National Archives, London, England, 2015.

Contents

Document type	Place/Title	Date From	Date To
Heading	WO95/2247-3 9th Bn Yorkshire Regt Sep 18 Feb 19		
Heading	9th Bn Yorkshire Regt Sep 1918-Feb 1919 From 23 Div 69 Bde and Italy Bde Div		
Heading	War Diary Of 9th Yorkshire Regiment From 1-9-18 To 31-9-18 (Volume 38)		
War Diary	Brusabo	01/09/1918	03/09/1918
War Diary	Reserve Trenches	10/09/1918	10/09/1918
War Diary	Centrlae	11/09/1918	12/09/1918
War Diary	Morano	13/09/1918	13/09/1918
War Diary	In Train	14/09/1918	17/09/1918
War Diary	St. Riquier Area	18/09/1918	26/09/1918
War Diary	Heilly	27/09/1918	28/09/1918
War Diary	Maricourt Area	29/09/1918	30/09/1918
Heading	War Diary For October 1918 Volume 39 9 Battalion Yorkshire Regt		
War Diary	Moislains	01/10/1918	18/10/1918
War Diary	Maretz	19/10/1918	31/10/1918
Operation(al) Order(s)	9th Yorkshire Regiment. Operation Order No. 56		
Miscellaneous	Warning Order	18/10/1918	18/10/1918
Miscellaneous	9th Yorkshire Regiment	19/10/1918	19/10/1918
Operation(al) Order(s)	9th Yorkshire Regiment Operation Order No. 1		
Miscellaneous	Appendix "A"		
Operation(al) Order(s)	9th Yorkshire Regiment Operation Order No. 2		
Miscellaneous	74th Infantry Brigade Instructions No.1	29/10/1918	29/10/1918
Heading	War Diary of 9th Yorkshire Regt From 1st November 1918 To 30th November 1918 Volume 40		
War Diary	Pommereuil	01/11/1918	12/11/1918
War Diary	Bousies	13/11/1918	13/11/1918
War Diary	Le Cateau	14/11/1918	30/11/1918
Miscellaneous	A Form Messages And Signals.		
Operation(al) Order(s)	74th Infantry Brigade Order No. 213	04/11/1918	04/11/1918
Operation(al) Order(s)	74th Infantry Brigade Order No 214	05/11/1918	05/11/1918
Miscellaneous	110 Brigade R.F.A.		
Miscellaneous	All Recipients of 74th Inf Bde Order No 214		
Heading	War Diary 9th Bn Yorkshire Regt From 1st Dec 1918 To 31st Dec 1918 Volume 41		
War Diary	St Vaast	01/12/1918	31/12/1918
Heading	War Diary Of 9th Bn Yorkshire Regt From 1st January 1919 To 31st January 1919 (Volume 41)		
War Diary	St Vaast	01/01/1919	18/01/1919
War Diary	Haussey	19/01/1919	31/01/1919
Heading	War Diary Of 9th Bn Yorkshire Regt Volume 42 From 1st February 1919 To 28th February 1919		
War Diary	Haussey	01/02/1919	18/02/1919
War Diary	Iwuy	19/02/1919	28/02/1919

WO95/2247/3

9th Bn Yorkshire Regt Sep 18 - Feb 19

25TH DIVISION
74TH INFY BDE

9TH BN YORKSHIRE REGT

SEP 1918-FEB 1919

from 23 DIV 69 Bde
and ITALY have DIV

— CONFIDENTIAL —

WAR DIARY

OF

9TH YORKSHIRE REGIMENT.

From 1-9-18. To 31-9-18.

(VOLUME 38)

Capt. & Adjt.
9th Yorkshire Regt.

Army Form C. 2118.

WAR DIARY
or
INTELLIGENCE SUMMARY.
(Erase heading not required.)

Instructions regarding War Diaries and Intelligence Summaries are contained in F. S. Regs., Part II. and the Staff Manual respectively. Title pages will be prepared in manuscript.

Place	Date	Hour	Summary of Events and Information	Remarks and references to Appendices
	SEPT/18			
BRUSABO	1st to 2nd		At BRUSABO CAMP. Carried out Gas Drill, Musketry, &c.	
RESERVE TRENCHES	3rd to 10th		Relieved 9th York & Lancs Regt and became Bn in Divisional Reserve. Bn carried out firing on Range.	
CENTRLAE	11th and 12th		Received orders to relieve 11th West Yorkshire Regt in Left Sub-Sector of Left Brigade Front, but same cancelled and Bn. moved to CENTRLAE to await orders for move to France.	
MORANO	13th		Moved to MORANO in afternoon, where "B" and "C" Coy entrained for France at 3·30 a.m on 14th, and "A" and "D" Coys at 7.30 a.m.	
IN TRAIN	14th to 17th		In train. Uneventful journey. Bn. detrained at ST. RIQUIER at 12.30 p.m and 2 p.m 17.9.18, respectively and marched to billets at NEUVILLE and ONEUX.	
ST. RIQUIER AREA	18th to 21st		In billets at NEUVILLE and ONEUX, where 25th Division was organised and consisted of 7th, 74th and 75th Infantry Brigades. Bn. together with 11th Sherwood Foresters and 13th Durham Light Infantry formed 7th Brigade. Training carried out and Bn organised to French Establishment. Transport moved by march route to HEILLY on 25th inst.	
HEILLY	27th and 28th		Bn. less transport entrained at ST RIQUIER at 12 noon and detrained at ALBERT about 6.30 p.m and marched to billets.	
MARICOURT AREA	29th and 30th		Bn. embussed and moved to Lutrenits and dugouts at FAVIERE WOOD in MARICOURT AREA.	

Casualties during month: O.Ranks

	KILLED	DIED OF WOUNDS	WOUNED
O.Ranks	1	2	9

Vol 39

Confidential

74/75

War Diary.

for

October 1918

Volume 39

9" Battalion
Yorkshire Regt

WAR DIARY
of
INTELLIGENCE SUMMARY.
(Erase heading not required.)

Army Form C. 2118.

Place	Date	Hour	Summary of Events and Information	Remarks and references to Appendices
NOISLAINS	1.10.18		In Hutments	NB
	3.10.18		Left MOISLAINS about 13.00 hours and marched to line S of LE CATELET	NB
	5.10.18		At 06.00 hours the Battalion commenced the attack on BEAUREVOIR but were held up by M.G. fire	NB
	6.10.18		After village had been captured by ROYAL WARWICKS the Battn. moved forward and dug in in front of village	NB
	8.10.18		Moved back to support position	NB
	9.10.18		At 02.30 hours moved forward through BEAUREVOIR to attack objective, reached and dug in on Eastern side of Railway near HONNECHY. After objective was reached cavalry pushed forward	NB
	10.10.18		Moved off to attack about 0200 hours and reached position 3 W. of S. BENIN where we dug in. Captured St BENIN about 1500 hours and dug in just outside the village.	NB
	12.10.18		Relieved by 2nd Bn Royal Munster Fusiliers and marched to HONNECHY	NB
	13.10.18		Moved to PREMONT	NB
	19.10.18		Moved to MARETZ	NB

WAR DIARY
or
INTELLIGENCE SUMMARY.
(Erase heading not required.)

Army Form C. 2118.

Place	Date	Hour	Summary of Events and Information	Remarks and references to Appendices
MARETZ	19.10.18		Stood to at 06.00 hours moved to HONNECHY at 13.00 hours	A
	18.10.18		moved off from HONNECHY at 03.00 hours Dug in E of LE CATEAU	B
			continued the advance about 09.00 hours Dug in on Edge of Bois	
			L'EVEQUE.	
	20.10.18		At 02.00 hours commenced the attack. Final objective reached & held	B
			Battn H.Q. in MALGANI. Bn. HQ. moved to FONTAINE AU BOIS.	
	21.10.18		Battn. took up new front line from G.14.b.60 to G.20.b.3.8 (BAR FOREST)	B
			One company in front line. One coy in support one coy in	
			MALGANI.	
	22.10.18		Relieved by 5th Gloucesters. Rest and moved back to billets in	B
			POMMEREUIL	
			Casualties for month.	
			Officers. Other ranks.	
			K. 6 63	
			W. 15 356	
			M. 41	

N Corner Capt Adj
for C.O. 9th Worc Regt

SECRET.   9TH YORKSHIRE REGIMENT.   Copy No...
  Ref.maps:-
Sh.57c.1/40000   OPERATION ORDERS No.56.
  62c.

1. The Bn. will move to MOISLAINS to-day, 1st October, and will be formed
   up with head of column on the road below H.Q.Mess, facing East, ready
   to move off at 10.30 hours in the following order :-
        H.Q. - "B"Coy - "C"Coy - Band - "A"Coy - "D"Coy.
   Distances of 100 yards will be maintained between Coys.

2. Transport will march in rear of the Bn. at 100 yards distance and
   distances of 25 yards will be maintained between each section of
   six vehicles.

3. Blankets will be stacked outside Q.M.Stores by 8 a.m.
   Officers kits and Mess boxes will be stacked outside the Q.M.Stores by
   9.30 a.m.

4. One Lorry has been allotted to carry blankets, stores etc. and will
   report at 8 a.m.

5. The usual billeting party will report to Lt.C.Read at the O.Room at
   8 a.m. Bicycles will be taken.

6. On arrival in new billets O.C.Coys will report 'All present' or
   otherwise.

   Distribution.
      No.1. C.O.   (sd) C.H.B.BOTTING.Capt.& Adjt.
         2. O.C."A"Coy.   9th Yorkshire Regiment.
         3. " "B" "
         4. " "C" "
         5. " "D" "
         6. T.O.
         7. Q.M.
         8. R.S.M.
         9. File.
        10. War Diary.

O.C. All Coys,
Q.M.
T.O.
R.S.M.

WARNING ORDER.

1. The Bn. will be ready to move off at 10 minutes after 0600 hrs. tomorrow the 19th inst.

2. All blankets will be returned to the Q.M. Stores by 0600, as also Officers kits and Mess boxes.

3. On receipt of code word 'ADVANCE' Coys will fall in on Main Road outside their billets.
   Pack animals loaded with Lewis Guns and ammunition in rear of respective Coys.
   Transport will parade in rear of the Bn.
   DRESS: Battle Order.

4. The Q.M. will make arrangements for the men to have Breakfast at 0530 hrs. tomorrow, and for an issue of tea at 0800 hrs should the Bn. not be required to move.

(sd) C.L. PORTER. Lieut. A/Adjt.
9th Yorkshire Regiment.

18/10/18.

Ref.map:- **9TH YORKSHIRE REGIMENT.**
Sheet 57b.

1. The Bn. will move to HONNECHY this afternoon and will be formed up with head on Main Road outside "A"Coy's H.Q.Billet at 1300 hrs, in the following order :-
    H.Q.Party - T.M.Section - "A"Coy - "B"Coy - "C"Coy - "B"Team - "X"Team - 1st & 2nd Line Transport.
The usual distances will be maintained on the march.

2. Pack animals loaded with Lewis Guns and ammunition will be in rear of respective Coys.

3. A Billeting Party of 1 N.C.O. par Coys and 1 for H.Q. will report to 2/Lt.L.J.Taylor forthwith. The party will subsequently report to the Staff Captain at HONNECHY CHURCH at 1100 hrs.

4. 1 blanket will be carried on the man.

5. Mess Boxes and officers kits will reach the Q.M.Stores by 1200 hrs.

6. The road will be kept clear to allow the 11th Sherwood Foresters and 13th D.L.I. to pass.

7. On arrival in Billets O.C.Coys will report 'All present' or otherwise.

19/10/18.

(sd) C.L.PORTER.Lieut.A/Adjt
9th Yorkshire Regiment

SECRET.   9TH YORKSHIRE REGIMENT   Copy No......

Ref.maps: parts of
57a, 57b, 62a. & 62b.
1/40,000

OPERATION ORDERS No. 1.

1. INFORMATION.	(Will be issued as the situation develops.) Two Tanks will co-operate with the Bn. after Zero plus 8. 13th D.L.I. will attack on Left, and 6th Division on Right. ~~A list of Tank Signals is in attached. (Appendix 'A').~~
2. INTENTIONS.	9th Yorkshire Regt. will seize the high ground running from G.14.a.central to G.14.c.0.2. - consolidate a line on the near slope, and push out outposts to line of Final objective.
3. INSTRUCTIONS.	
(a)	The Bn. will be formed up along the road running from L.15.d.7.4. to L.29.a.5.5. in column of route by Zero plus 6½ hours in the following order :- "B"Coy - "C"Coy - "D"Coy - H.Qrs. and will advance North East through BOIS L'EVEQUE, and be formed up ready to pass through the RED LINE at Zero plus 8.
(b)	"B" Company on the Right - "C" Company on the Left. "A" Company in Support. Dividing Line between Coys - a line running from the Northern Houses of MALGARNI (L.18.c.6.4.) to G.14.b.2.5.
(c)	There will be an Army Barrage on a line running from L.13.a.central to L.13.c.8.0. until Zero plus 10 hrs. 12 minutes.
(d)	The Bn. will consolidate in depth behind this barrage prior to advancing to Final Objective at Zero plus 10 hrs. 12 minutes.
(e)	O.C."A" Coy will detail 1 Lewis Gun Section as escorts for Tanks, and to report to Officer in charge of same at cross roads L.24.a.2.2.
(f)	A list of Tank Signals is attached.(Appendix 'A'). These signals will be explained to all ranks.
4. AID POSTS.	Will be established as below :- First at vicinity of road junction L.24.b.1.1. Later in MALGARNI. Finally :- cross roads L.12.a.8.6.
5. REPORT CENTRE.	Reports will be forwarded :- First to road junction L.24.b.1.1. Secondly (after Zero plus 10 hrs 12 min.) to MALGARNI. Thirdly. After objective has been taken to cross roads L.12.a.8.6.
6. ZERO HOUR.	Will be notified later.
7. COMPASS BEARING.	General direction of advance from Zero plus 8. - 65°True.

22/10/18.

Lieut. Colonel.
Commanding 9th Yorkshire Regt.

Distribution.
No. 1. Filed.
2. O.C."A"Coy.
3. " "B" "
4. " "C" "
5. M.O.
6. War Diary.
7. S.O.
8. CO
9. Maj-Gen Humphries
10. Adjt

APPENDIX 'A'.

The following are the signals used by the Tank Corps in action:-

A GREEN and WHITE Flag flown by Tank = Come on.

A RED and YELLOW Flag flown by Tank. = Disabled.

A RED, WHITE & BLUE Flag flown by Tank = Coming out. (In order to show that the Tank is British.

    If the Infantry are held up and wish for the assistance of Tanks, a helmet on the end of a rifle will be pointed in the direction of trouble. The same signal is used by the Tank Corps when they require assistance from the Infantry.

    British Tanks are marked RED, WHITE and BLUE in Front and Rear.

    German Tanks are marked with a BLACK CROSS.

SECRET.   9TH YORKSHIRE REGIMENT   Copy No......
Ref.maps:-
sheet 57a.57b.   OPERATION ORDERS No.2.

1. The Bn. will be formed up with head at Cross roads P.30.a.3.2. ready
   to move off at 0030 hrs in the following order :-
        "B"Coy - "C"Coy - "A"Coy - H.Q. & Section of 74th L.T.M.B.
   Pack mules with Lewis Guns and ammunition in rear of Coys etc.-
   "A"Echelon Transport in rear of Bn.

2. Route:- LE CATEAU - Road junction Q.4.b.5.0. - cross roads K.34.d.9.6.-
           K.35.d.6.0. - L.31.b.1.2. - road junction L.26.d.0.4. - cross
           roads L.20.central - L.15.d.5.4.

3. The usual distances will be maintained during the march.
   Coys will be ready to open out in platoons at 50 yards interval if
   required.

4. The Q.M. will arrange for a hot meal for the Bn. at 2300 hrs. and will
   also arrange that the men carry with them tomorrows rations which must
   be cooked in advance.

5. A halt will be made in the vicinity of Q.10.central, where hot tea and
   rum will be issued under arrangements to be made by the Q.M.
   A second halt will be made in the vicinity of L.31.b. and a third halt
   near L.20.a.

6. The Cookers will not proceed beyond Q.10.b. but will come under orders
   of the Staff Captain.

7. "B"Echelon Transport, blankets etc. will remain in HONNECHY.

8. All kits, blankets etc. will be dumped at the Q.M.Stores not later
   than 2200 hrs.

9. 2/Lt.E.H.Warham will report at Brigade H.Q. at 2300 hrs. to synchronise
   watches, which he will collect from the Adjutant.
   Watches will be synchronised by Coy Commanders at 2330 hrs.

10. The Bn. will move from HONNECHY in Battle order i.e.complete with
    S.O.S.Rockets, Bombs, Flares etc. also billhooks which will be issued
    to the leading 4 platoons of the Bn.

22/10/18.   (sd) C.L.PORTER.Lieut.A/Adjt.
Distribution.   9th Yorkshire Regiment.
   No.1. File.
      2. O.C."A"Coy.
      3. "   "B" "
      4. "   "C" "
      5. M.O.
      6. S.O.
      7. War Diary.
      8. C.O.
      9. Major G.N.Hunnybun.
     10. Adjutant.
     11. T.O.
     12. Q.M.

S E C R E T.   Copy No 4

74th Infantry Brigade Instructions No. ~~X~~

Reference Sheets FOREST
& 57a N.W. 1/20,000   29th October 1918.

1. The 25th Division will be prepared to carry out an operation on the morning of October 30th on receipt of orders today. The Object of this Operation is to secure ground in advance of the Line now held to facilitate forthcoming operations.

2. The Objective to be captured by the Division will be as follows:-
Road between G.20.b.4.9. and G.21.a.7.9. - G.15.d.6.8.(on Light Railway) - G.15.b.6.3. (where Railway crosses FONTAINE AU BOIS - LANDRECIES Road) - G.15.b.8.7. - G.9.c.8.5. - G.9.c.1.9. to present Line at G.8.b.5.3.

3. The attack will be carried out by 74th Infantry Brigade on the RIGHT and 75th Infantry Brigade on the LEFT. The 7th Infantry Brigade will swing forward its Right to link up with the Left of the 75th Infantry Brigade at G.9.c.1.9.

4. <u>DIVIDING LINE between BRIGADES.</u>
LANDRECIES-FONTAINE AU BOIS Road running through G.15.b. - G.9.c. - G.8.d. inclusive to 75th Infantry Brigade.

5. <u>DETAIL.</u> (a) The 9th Yorkshire Regt will be on the RIGHT.
          (b) The 11th Sherwood Foresters will be on the LEFT.
          (c) The 13th Durham Light Infantry will be in support and at ZERO minus 2 hours will move to the vicinity of G.13.d. where they will dig in, and be ready to support either 9th Yorks or 11th S.F.

6. <u>ASSEMBLY POSITION.</u> Battalions will assemble on Line North and South Grid Line running through G.14.central from G.20.b.0.6. - G.8.d.00.25. Tape will be laid out on this Line under Brigade arrangements. Battalions will see that they have gaps made in hedges through which they will pass from Assembly Position to present Front Line. No posts will be EAST of forming up Tape at ZERO minus 2 hours.

7. <u>BARRAGE.</u> The Attack will be carried out under a creeping barrage. The Barrage will come down at ZERO on a line one hundred yards West of the North and South Grid Line between G.14. and G.15 and will remain for 6 minutes when it will commence to move forward at the Rate of 100 yards in 6 minutes. A protective barrage will be put down beyond the FINAL OBJECTIVE, which will remain for 30 minutes after the time allowed for the capture of FINAL OBJECTIVE.

8. <u>SYNCHRONISATION OF WATCHES.</u> Brigade Signalling Officer will arrange to send 2 Watches to Battalions to have reached last Battalion Headquarter by 05.00

9. <u>MACHINE GUNS.</u> One Section of 25th Bn. M.Gun Corps is allotted to the Brigade. 2 Guns will take up a position at G.20.b.4.7. where they will remain. Remaining 2 Guns will cover the Advance. When the Objective has been reached these 2 guns will take up a position about G.21.a.7.9.

10. <u>ZERO HOUR.</u> ZERO Hour will be 08.00 October 30th 1918.

11. A C K N O W L E D G E.   *[signature]*

                                                                            Captain.
Issued through Signals   Brigade Major   74th Infantry Brigade.
at _____

Copies to :-
No. 1	25th Division G.	No. 4	9th Yorks Regt.	8	330 Bde R.F.A.
2	75th Inf.Brigade.	5	11th Sher.For.	9	25th Bn.M.G.C.
3	16th Inf.Brigade.	6	13th D.L.I.	10	Brigade I.O.
		7	74th T.M.B.	11	Bde Sig. Officer.

Confidential

War Diary

of

9th Yorkshire Regt.

From 1st November 1917
to 30th November 1918

Volume 40

Volume 40

Army Form C. 2118.

WAR DIARY
or
INTELLIGENCE SUMMARY.
(*Erase heading not required.*)

Instructions regarding War Diaries and Intelligence Summaries are contained in F. S. Regs., Part II. and the Staff Manual respectively. Title pages will be prepared in manuscript.

Place	Date	Hour	Summary of Events and Information	Remarks and references to Appendices
POMMEREUIL	1/11/18		In billets at POMMEREUIL	8/6/1
"	2.11.18		In billets at POMMEREUIL	8/6/2
"	3.11.18		In billets at POMMEREUIL	
	4.11.18	0500	Moved off from POMMEREUIL and took up positions outside MAIRIEUX. Very misty morning and positions reached without being observed. 0100 Bn moved from MALGRAIN towards LANDRECIES. Showed forward advance guard to Brigade. No opposition encountered. Shelling of importance 400 hours across river at LANDRECIES by means of Petrol tin floatbridge look out post line with HQ at a farm which had been enemy artillery HQ. One battery & 2 hows on 8" how + 8 prisoners taken.	8/6/3
	5.11.18		Moved off about 0900 hours. 19th Middlesex formed advance guard to 9th Bde at OLD MILL DESTREE Brigade. Crossed PETITE HELPE River. Slight opposition encountered. Slight opposition at MAROILLES. Village occupied and outpost line taken up astride MAIRBAIX mainroad.	
	6.11.18		9th N'hots Regt formed advance guard. "A" Coy under Capt W.L. BLOW.	etc.

WAR DIARY
or
INTELLIGENCE SUMMARY.
(Erase heading not required.)

Army Form C. 2118.

Place	Date	Hour	Summary of Events and Information	Remarks and references to Appendices
	6.11.18		Van guard slight opposition also mauned one troop cavalry and two armoured cars operated with us. Held up by M.G. fire on left angle of road before MAIRBAIX. MAIRBAIX occupied by "A" + "C" Coys about 1400 hours. Had a running fight with enemy but could not come in close contact with him. 5 Prisoners and eight M.G. taken in MAIRBAIX. Enemy shelled village slightly about 1630 hours. Outpost line taken up outside village.	E.M.
	7.11.18		4th 13 Inf Bde passed thro us & continued the advance. 9th Yorks who were in billets in MAIRBAIX at 1500 hours marched back to MAROILLES where stayed for night.	E.M.
	8.11.18		moved back to billets at BOUSIES.	E.M.
	9.11.18		In billets at BOUSIES.	E.M.
	10.11.18		In billets at BOUSIES.	E.M.
	11.11.18		In billets at BOUSIES. Hostilities with GERMANY ceased at 1100 hours	E.M.
	12.11.18		In billets at BOUSIES.	

Army Form C. 2118.

WAR DIARY
or
INTELLIGENCE SUMMARY.
(Erase heading not required.)

Instructions regarding War Diaries and Intelligence Summaries are contained in F. S. Regs. Part II. and the Staff Manual respectively. Title pages will be prepared in manuscript.

Place	Date	Hour	Summary of Events and Information	Remarks and references to Appendices
BOUSIES	13/11/18	10.00	Moved to billets in LE CATEAU. Arrived LE CATEAU at 13.30 hours	2/n.
LE CATEAU	14/11/18		Party of 58 others ranks arrived. In billets at LE CATEAU	2/n.
"	15/11/18		In billets at LE CATEAU	2/n.
"	16/11/18		In billets at LE CATEAU	2/n.
"	17/11/18		In billets at LE CATEAU	2/n.
"	18/11/18		In billets at LE CATEAU	6/n.
"	19/11/18		In billets at LE CATEAU	6/n.
"	20/11/18		In billets at LE CATEAU. Salvage operations commenced. Two companies	
"	21/11/18		all day on Salvage, two companies training till Sports to	6/n.
"	22/11/18		Head Q'rs & Army Area	
"	23/11/18		In billets at LE CATEAU	6/n.
"	24/11/18		In billets at LE CATEAU	6/n.
"	25/11/18		In billets at LE CATEAU	2/n.
"	26/11/18			

Army Form C. 2118.

WAR DIARY
or
INTELLIGENCE SUMMARY.
(Erase heading not required.)

Instructions regarding War Diaries and Intelligence Summaries are contained in F. S. Regs., Part II. and the Staff Manual respectively. Title pages will be prepared in manuscript.

Place	Date	Hour	Summary of Events and Information	Remarks and references to Appendices
27.11.18			In billets in LE CATEAU	S/M
28.11.18				S/M
29.11.18		9.00	moved to billets in St VAAST	S/M
	30/11/18		In billets in St VAAST	
			Casualties for month	
			Killed Wounded missing	
			Officers nil nil nil	
			Othr ranks 3 32 15	
				H. Bowman Capt a/Adjt for OC 9 Yorks Regt

"A" Form
MESSAGES AND SIGNALS.

Army Form C. 2121
(In pads of 100.)

TO: 9 Yorks. 11 Sher For. 13 DLI. 25 Div G. 110 Bde LH.

Sender's Number: BM 11 Day of Month: 4

50 Divn are in B.26 central aaa. The Brigade will advance at once and take up the line BOUILLETTE FM H.26 a through H.8/0 central & LEFT CATILLON FM H.14 a 9 Yorks will hold line from LANDRECIES–MAROILLES Rd inclusive to CATILLON FM (inclusive) and 11 Sher Foresters LANDRECIES MAROILLES Rd (exclusive) to BOUILLETTE FM (inclusive) aaa This position must be held in depth with outpost line well forward on Eastern slopes and all roads leading Eastwards will be picketed aaa 13 DLI will be in Support about H.10 central

"A" Form
MESSAGES AND SIGNALS.

Army Form C. 2121
(In pads of 100.)

(circled: M-70 aaa)

aaa The 75 Inf Bde will guard the Right Flank from about H 25 central - SAULEBRUANTE (G30 b) and Glassworks in G35 b aaa The 7 Inf Bde will be in reserve with one Battn holding RED LINE and 2 Bns Railway Line aaa Brigade HQr will move to vicinity of G23d on LANDRECIES - MAROILLES Road aaa Parties will be pushed out by 9 Yorks from CATILLON F.M. to seize if possible bridgehead at OLD MILL DES PRES aaa 1 Shr for. will push parties out to seize if possible Bridgeheads

"A" Form
MESSAGES AND SIGNALS.

Army Form C. 2121
(In pads of 100.)

in neighbourhood H16 central aaa Patrols must be sent out as soon as line has been reached Patrols will be sent out to get in touch with 50 Divn on left + 75 Bde on right aaa no movement forward after 17.30 aaa Bns will report exact dispositions to Bde HQr aaa ACKNOWLEDGE

From: 74 Bde
Place:
Time: 3.30 hrs

"A" Form
MESSAGES AND SIGNALS.

Army Form C. 2121
(In pads of 160.)

Prefix....Code....m	words	Charge	This message is on a/c	Recd. at....m
Office of Origin and Service Instructions				
	Sent		....Service	Date....
17-30	At....m			From....
	To		(Signature of "Franking Officer")	By....
	By			

TO 9th Yorks —

Sender's Number	Day of Month	In reply to Number	AAA
BM 6	4		

Parties of 1/5 Gloucesters and 1/8 Worcesters reported to have crossed CANAL - aaa RIGHT Company of WORCESTERS crossed by Bridge S.E. of G 22 central aaa Centre & Reserve Companies of Worcesters following by same crossing aaa No report from Left Company of WORCESTERS who were pushing on to seize main crossing in G23 a aaa 11th Sherwood Foresters have been ordered to push across CANAL to support 75th Inf Bde to establish RED LINE and if possible RED.DOTTED.LINE

From
Place
Time

The above may be forwarded as now corrected (Z)

Censor. Signature of Addressor or person authorised to telegraph in his name
* This line should be erased if not required.

Order No. 1625   Wt. W3253/   P 511   27/2   H. & K. Ltd. (E. 2634).

"A" Form
MESSAGES AND SIGNALS.

Army Form C. 2121
(In pads of 100.)

Prefix......Code.......m.	words	Charge	This message is on a/c :	Recd. at......m.
Office of Origin and Service Instructions	Sent		................Service.	Date..........
	At ....m.			From ....
	To			
	By		(Signature of "Franking Officer")	By............

TO		2		
	Sender's Number.	Day of Month.	In reply to Number.	**A A A**

9th Yorks & 13 DLI will be prepared to cross CANAL SE of G22 central on receipt of orders. aaa when ordered to cross CANAL they will be prepared to take over the RED DOTTED LINE (OUTPOST LINE) aaa acknowledge Foot bridge in G22a reported intact aaa

From: 74 Inf Bde
Place:
Time: 1150

The above may be forwarded as now corrected (Z)

Censor. Signature of Addressor or person authorised to telegraph in his name.
* This line should be erased if not required.

Order No. 1625 Wt. W3253/ P 511 27/2 H. & K., Ltd. (E. 2634).

S E C R E T.   Copy No

           74th   INFANTRY   BRIGADE   ORDER   No.213.

Reference Sheets 57a 1/40,000
& 57a N.W. 1/20,000   4th November 1918.

1. The Advance will be continued tomorrow November 5th 1918.

2. ADVANCED GUARD.
   Brigadier General H.M.CRAIGIE-HALKETT DSO) will Advance at
      74th Infantry Brigade.   ) 06.15 hours and
      110th Brigade R.F.A.   ) will make good
      130th Field Co R.E.   ) the following
      1 Troop 12th Lancers.   ) Objectives -

   (a) The GREEN LINE described in 74th Infantry Brigade Instruction
       No. 1 para 2 SERIES "A".
   (b) The Line J.19.a.0.0. - Cross Roads J.7.central - Cross Roads
       J.2.a.2.6.

3. VANGUARD & MAINGUARD.
   Lieut.Col. CARROLL M.C. Officer Commanding.
   (11th Sherwood Foresters.).
   2 Sections 12th Lancers.
   1 Section 130th Field Company R.E.
   11th Sherwood Foresters..

4. ROUTE. - LE PRESEAU - H.19.a. - LABLANCHISSERIE - H.18.d. -
   CATILLON EM H.14.a. - OLD MILL DES PRES H.8.b.7.6. - RUE DE JUIFS
   H.4.c.90.35 (Road junction) - Cross Road H.11.c.2.6. - H.6.central -
   NOYELLES C.25.d.3.8. then NOYELLES - PETIT MAUBEUGE Road.

5. STARTING POINT. Head of MAIN GUARD will pass Road junction H.19.a.8.3
   at 06.15 tomorrow November 5th.

6. ORDER OF MARCH of MAIN BODY.
             9th Yorkshire Regt.
             13th Durham Light Infantry.
             'A' Company 25th Bn M.Gun Corps.
             130th Field Company R.E.(Less 1 Section).
             110th Brigade R.F.A.
   Main body will Not pass Road junction G.30.b.0.9. until main guard
   has reported high Ground in H.14. clear of enemy.

7. DISTANCES. -   50 yards between Platoons.
                  100 yards between Companies.
                  800 yards between Battalions and Other Units.

8. ARTILLERY. 110, 112, and 150 Brigades R.F.A. will cover the Advance.
   'A' Battery 110 Brigade R.F.A. (under Captain Radcliffe) will get into
   touch with Officer Commanding Main Guard (Lieut Col CORRALL) and will
   push his Battery forward to cover any opposition.
   As soon as High Ground in H.14. had been made good 110 Brigade R.F.A.
   will be prepared to move forward on receipt of Orders and Advance behind
   Brigade.

9. CAVALRY. Cavalry will move to vicinity of G.23.c. (S of Landrecies)
   tonight November 4/5th.
   2 Sections move with Main Guards 1 troop (less 2 sections) under 2/Lt
   RICHARDS will move with Brigade Headquarters.   2/Lt Richards will
   report to Brigade Headquarters 1 hour before ZERO.

10. R.E's. (a) 130th Field Company R.E. will move to vicinity of G.23.c.
    South of LANDRECIES tonight Nov. 4/5th.
           (b) 2 Cork Bridges of 130th Field Co R.E. on Pontoon Wagons
    will be parked in G.24.c. ready to move forward immediately on receipt
    of orders.   Remainder of Pontoons will remain in G.23.c. until ordered
    to move forward.
    In the event of Bridge at (i) OLD MILL DES PRES H.9.a.1.7. (b) H.16.b.
    being destroyed -

(2)

being destroyed orders will be issued to O.C. 130th Field Company R.E to move up 2 Cork Bridges on Pontoon Wagons and throw Bridges across to pass over Infantry.
O.C. 130th Field Company R.E. will report to Brigade Headquarters 1 hour before ZERO.

11. MACHINE GUNS. One Company ('A') 25th Bn M.Gun Corps will move in rear of 13th Durham Light Infantry in limbers. O.C. Company to report to Brigade Headquarters 1 hour before ZERO.

12. BRIGADE HEADQUARTERS. Brigade Headquarters will move to G.23.d.00.85 and will open there at 04.00 Nov. 5th 1918.

13. PRESENT LOCATION OF UNITS.

   9th Yorkshire Regt. G.24.b.5.4.
   11th Sherwood Foresters G.30.b.1.9.
   13th D.L.I.   G.22.c.6.3.
   'A' Co 25th Bn M.G.C. G.23.d 00.85.

14. PONTOON BRIDGES. across CANAL have been made at -
  (a) about 400 yards N.E. of Main Landrecies Bridge.
  (b) " 200 yards S.W. of Main Landrecies Bridge.

15. BOUNDARIES.
Northern Boundary as shewn on Map 57a N.W. 1/20,000 issued with 74th Infantry Brigade Instruction No. 1 Series A.
Southern Boundary. LANDRECIES - MARBAIX Road.

16. The 75th Infantry Brigade will provide Right Flank protection in the event of 32nd Division not having come up level with the 25th Division. 75th Infantry Brigade will keep pace with the Advance of the 74th Infantry Brigade.

17. A C K N O E L E D G E.

                 [signature]
                 Captain.
         Brigade Major 74th Infantry Brigade.

Issued through Signals
at   01-00

   No. 1 25th Division G.
     2 9th Yorkshire Regt.
     3 11th Sherwood Foresters.
     4 13th Durham Light Infantry.
     5 110 Brigade R.F.A.
     6 'A' Co 25th Bn M.G.C.
     7 75th Infantry Brigade.
     8 7th Infantry Brigade.
     9 130 Field Company R.E.
    10 No. 1 Troop B Squad 12th Lancers.
    11 Staff Captain.

SECRET.   Copy No 2

74TH INFANTRY BRIGADE ORDER No. 214

Ref Sheet 57a N.W. 1/20,000   5th November 1918

1. **SITUATION.** Pockets of enemy with Machine Guns and Trench Mortars being rounded up in vicinity of VALLEZ Fm. H.12.d. and H.11.b.7.3.

2. The Brigade will take up an Outpost Line for night 5/6th November running from Road junction H.5.c.0.7. - along Track to Cross Roads H.11.b.1.3 - to Cross Roads H.11.d.8.6. - Road junction H.18.a.8.6. then through H.18.central to Southern Divisional Boundary (H.18.d.3.6).
SUPPORT LINE approximately along GREEN LINE.

3. **DISPOSITIONS.** The OUTPOST Line will be held by

    11th Sherwood Foresters on RIGHT.
    9th Yorkshire Regt.   CENTRE
    13th Durham L.Inf on   LEFT.

    Each Battalion will hold the OUTPOST Line with one Company - 2 Companies of each Battalion will be in billets in close Support.

4. **BOUNDARIES.** RIGHT BATTALION (11th Sherwood Foresters) H.18.d.3.6. (inclusive) - H.12.c.4.1. -
CENTRE BATTALION (9th Yorkshire Regt) H.12.c.4.1. - H.11.b.1.3 (inclusive).
LEFT BATTALION (13th Durham L.Inf) H.11.b.1.3. (exclusive) - H.5.c.0.7. (Cross Tracks - inclusive).

5. **BRIGADE HEADQUARTERS.** LA BLANCHISSERIE FM H.13.d.4.4. Advanced Report Centre CATILLON Farm.

    BATTN H.Q.
    11th Sherwood Foresters about H.17.a.9.7.
    9th Yorkshire Regt   about H.11.c.1.8.
    13th Durham Light Infantry about H.4.c.8.4.

6. 7th Infantry Brigade will be in Billets RUE DE LIEUTENANT unless orders are issued to the contrary by G.O.C. 7th Infantry Brigade.

7. 110th Brigade R.F.A. have taken up position East of PETITE HELPE to cover the Advance of the Brigade tomorrow November 6th.

8. 'A' Company 25th Bn M.G.C will arrange covering fire in front of OUTPOST LINE.

9. **PATROLS.** All Roads and Tracks leading East from Our Positions must be patrolled. Patrols will also get into touch with 50th Division on LEFT and with 75th Inf Bde or 32nd Divn on RIGHT.

10. A C K N O W L E D G E.

                                                      Captain.
                                        Brigade Major 74th Infantry Bde.

Issued through
Signals at 16.30
        Copied to
            No 1 25th Divn   No 4 13th Durham L.Inf.
               2 9th Yorkshire Regt.   5 'A' Co 25th Bn M.G.C.
               3 11th Sherwood For.   6 110 Brigade R.F.A.
                    7 File.

110 Brigade R.F.A.
9th Yorkshire Regt.
11th Sherwood Foresters.
13th Durham Light Infantry.

M.19   5th.

21st Manchesters (7th Infantry Brigade) and parties of 50th Division reported in BASSE NOYELLE AAA Artillery S.O.S. Line for night 5/6th November will be on a Line I.13.central to H.12 central AAA North of latter point No Artillery fire West of GRANDE HAIE RAU AAA Please notify 35th Divisional Artillery and all Batteries concerned AAA ACKNOWLEDGE AAA Addressed 110 Brigade R.F.A. repeated 9th Yorkshire Regt 11th Sherwood Foresters and 13th Durham Light Infantry

Captain.
Brigade Major 74th Infantry Brigade.

To.-
All Recipients of 74th Inf Bde Order No. 214.

M.20   5th.

Reference Brigade Order No.214 AAA Since this Order was issued 21st Manchesters have taken BASSE NOYELLES and 9th Yorkshire Regt has taken RUE DES HAIES AAA In consequence of this the 15th Durham Light Infantry will be withdrawn from the OUTPOST LINE and move into Billets in RUE DESJUIFS and RUE DES SABLONNIERES at once AAA ACKNOWLEDGE.

Captain.
Brigade Major 74th Infantry Brigade.

Issued through Signals.
at 18.30

CONFIDENTIAL WAR DIARY

9TH BN. YORKSHIRE REGT.

From 1st Dec. 1918 To 31st Dec 1918

Volume IV.

.... Capt. A/Adjt.
For O.C. 9th Yorks Regt.

Army Form C. 2118.

WAR DIARY
or
INTELLIGENCE SUMMARY.
(Erase heading not required.)

Volume 41.

Instructions regarding War Diaries and Intelligence Summaries are contained in F. S. Regs., Part II. and the Staff Manual respectively. Title pages will be prepared in manuscript.

Place	Date	Hour	Summary of Events and Information	Remarks and references to Appendices
St Vaast	1/7/18		In billets at St Vaast. Salvage work continued.	
	2/7/18		ditto	
	3/7/18		ditto	
	4/7/18		ditto	
	5/7/18		ditto	
	6/7/18		ditto	
	7/7/18		ditto	
	8/7/18		ditto	
	9/7/18		ditto	
	10/7/18		ditto	
	11/7/18		ditto	
	12/7/18		ditto	
	13/7/18		ditto	
	14/7/18		ditto	
	15/7/18		ditto	
	16/7/18		ditto	

Army Form C. 2118.

WAR DIARY
or
INTELLIGENCE SUMMARY.
(Erase heading not required.)

Instructions regarding War Diaries and Intelligence Summaries are contained in F. S. Regs., Part II. and the Staff Manual respectively. Title pages will be prepared in manuscript.

Place	Date	Hour	Summary of Events and Information	Remarks and references to Appendices
ST VAAST	16/12/18		In Billet at ST VAAST	
	18/12/18		— ditto —	
	19/12/18		— ditto —	
	20/12/18		— ditto —	
	21/12/18		— ditto —	
	22/12/18		— ditto —	
	23/12/18		— ditto —	
	24/12/18		— ditto — Holiday	
	25/12/18		— ditto — -ditto-	
	26/12/18		— ditto — -ditto-	
	27/12/18		— ditto —	
	28/12/18		— ditto —	
	29/12/18		— ditto —	
	30/12/18		— ditto —	
	31/12/18		— ditto —	

Major
for O.C. 19 v Yorkshire Regt

CONFIDENTIAL

WAR DIARY No 42

OF

9TH BN YORKSHIRE REGT.

FROM 1ST JANUARY 1919 TO 31ST JANUARY 1919

(VOLUME 41.)

Army Form C. 2118.

WAR DIARY
or
INTELLIGENCE SUMMARY.
(Erase heading not required.)

Instructions regarding War Diaries and Intelligence [Summaries] Summaries are contained in F. S. Regs., Part II. and the Staff Manual respectively. Title pages will be prepared in manuscript.

Place	Date	Hour	Summary of Events and Information	Remarks and references to Appendices
St VAAST	1/1/19		In billets at St VAAST	
	2/1/19		do	
	3/1/19		do	
	4/1/19		do	
	5/1/19		do	
	6/1/19		do	
	7/1/19		do	
	8/1/19		do	
	9/1/19		do	
	10/1/19		do	
	11/1/19		do	
	12/1/19		do	
	13/1/19		do	1 other rank demobilized
	14/1/19		do	
	15/1/19		do	3 other ranks demobilized

(A7853) Wt. W809/M1072 350,000 4/17 D. D. & L., London, E.C. **Sch. 52a.** Forms/C/2118/14

Army Form C. 2118.

WAR DIARY
or
INTELLIGENCE SUMMARY.

(Erase heading not required.)

Instructions regarding War Diaries and Intelligence Summaries are contained in F. S. Regs., Part II. and the Staff Manual respectively. Title pages will be prepared in manuscript.

Place	Date	Hour	Summary of Events and Information	Remarks and references to Appendices
SIVCOST	14/1/19	—	In hillet at 5" Vaast 130 other ranks demobilized	2pm
" "	18/1/19	11 oclock	moved to billets in HAUSSEY 10 other ranks demobilized.	8pm.
HAUSSEY	19/1/19	—	In billets at HAUSSEY.	5pm.
"	20/1/19	—	do	5pm
"	21.1.19	—	do 130 other ranks demobilized	6pm
"	22.1.19	—	do 9 other ranks demobilized	6pm
"	23.1.19	—	do 13 other ranks demobilized	6pm
"	24.1.19	—	do 15 other ranks demobilized.	6pm
"	25.1.19	—	do 10 other ranks demobilized 1 officer demobilized	6pm
"	26.1.19	—	do 1 officer demobilized	6pm
"	27.1.19	—	do 13 other ranks demobilized	6pm
"	28.1.19	—	do 12 other ranks demobilized	6pm
"	29.1.19	—	do 12 other ranks demobilized	6pm
"	30.1.19	10.30	The King's Colours were consecrated, presented & trooped. Major JENKIN C.F. consecrated the colour and this was presented by Major-General T.R.E. CHARLES.C.B.D.S.O. 2pm. The colour was received by Lieut. J.S. WOOD.M.C. Lieut-Col. R.S.HART. D.S.O. was in command of the guard. Present at the ceremony were Brig. Genl. H.M CRAIGIE - HALKETT. C.M.G. D.S.O. + Lt. Colonel ANDERSON. 19 other ranks demobilized.	
	31.1.19	—	In billets at HAUSSEY. 19 other ranks demobilized.	6pm

Mille Crosby Major
for O.C. 9° Yorks Regt

Confidential

War Diary
of
9° Bn Yorkshire Regt

Volume 42

From 1st February 1919
To 28° February 1919

Volume N°2

WAR DIARY
or
INTELLIGENCE SUMMARY.
(Erase heading not required.)

Army Form C. 2118.

Instructions regarding War Diaries and Intelligence Summaries are contained in F. S. Regs., Part II. and the Staff Manual respectively. Title pages will be prepared in manuscript.

Place	Date	Hour	Summary of Events and Information	Remarks and references to Appendices
HAUSSY	1.2.19		In billets at Haussey	2/hr.
"	2.2.19		In billets at Haussey - 15 other ranks proceeded for demobilisation	6/hr.
"	3.2.19	"	" 38 "	2/hr.
"	4.2.19	"	" "	2/hr.
"	5.2.19	"	" "	6/hr.
"	6.2.19	"	" "	6/hr.
"	7.2.19	"	" 36 other ranks proceeded for demobilisation	2/hr.
"	8.2.19	"	" 25 "	18/hr.
"	9.2.19	"	" 2 officers & 2 Y.O.R.	2/hr.
"	10.2.19	"	" 1 " 15 "	6/hr.
"	11.2.19	"	" 1 " 1 "	6/hr.
"	12.2.19	"	" 10 other ranks proceeded for demobilisation	8/hr.
"	13.2.19	"	" 6 "	2/hr.
"	14.2.19	"	" 3 "	16/hr.
"	15.2.19	"	" 11 " (r.c. officer)	12/hr.
"	16.2.19	"	" 1 "	8/hr.

WAR DIARY
or
INTELLIGENCE SUMMARY.
(Erase heading not required.)

Army Form C. 2118.

Place	Date	Hour	Summary of Events and Information	Remarks and references to Appendices
HOUSSEY	17.2.19	—	In billet at HOUSSEY. Other ranks proceeded to demobilization	8/hr.
"	18.2.19	9.30	Move of G billets in INUY. arrived at 1300 hours	8/hr.
INUY	19.2.19	—	In billets at INUY. 10 other ranks proceeded to demobilization	8/hr.
"	20.2.19	—	" " 2 " " "	8/hr.
"	21.2.19	—	" " 3 " " "	8/hr.
"	22.2.19	—	" " (+ 1 officer)	8/hr.
"	23.2.19	—	" " 1 officer + 10 O.R.	8/hr.
"	24.2.19	—	" " 4 other ranks "	8/hr.
"	25.2.19	—	" " 1 " "	8/hr.
"	26.2.19	—	" " " " "	
"	27.2.19	—	" " " " "	
"	28.2.19	—	10 other ranks proceeded for demobilization	8/hr.

Sharland, a/Adjt
for O.C. 9 ey/o/p Regt

www.ingramcontent.com/pod-product-compliance
Lightning Source LLC
Chambersburg PA
CBHW081248170426
43191CB00037B/2077